Fashion Illustration: Flat Drawing

p

Fashion Illustration: Flat Drawing

Copyright © 2007 Parragon Books Ltd

Parragon Books Ltd
Queen Street House
4 Queen Street
Bath BA1 1HE, UK

Produced by Loft
Illustrations: Elena Sáez and Maite Lafuente
Text: Aitana Lleonart and Daniela Santos
Editorial coordinator: Catherine Collin
Art director: Mireia Casanovas Soley
Layout: Emma Termes Parera

English edition produced by Cambridge Publishing Management Ltd
Translator: Cynthia Stephens
Copy-editor: Sandra Stafford

ISBN: 978-1-4054-9809-8

Printed in China

Index

FLAT DRAWING

Within the world of fashion illustration there exists a discipline that is characterized by practical schematization and visualization of articles of clothing: flat drawing. Despite its apparent simplicity, to be able to capture all the details of the costumes one needs to be aware of certain aspects that are sometimes forgotten and that lend an article the distinctive characteristic that differentiates it from the rest.

The objective of this book is to provide the reference points and necessary variations for learning to draw plane designs for fashion in a simple and progressive manner. The advantage of this discipline is that it is not necessary to create human figures on which to illustrate the clothing, something that can become a complicated task depending on a person's skills. This book is directed at creative people who are not keen on drawing fashion models, and offers them the possibility of representing their ideas in a basic and functional manner without the necessity of applying them to the human body.

To start well it is necessary to remember a key concept of flat drawing for fashion: symmetry. The first step is to establish the axes of the structure: even though the garment includes asymmetric finishes, it is essential to represent each garment (shirts, coats, jackets, trousers or skirts) in a proportional manner starting from the central axis. This book provides, through its many examples, the tools necessary for achieving proportionality and coherence for all of the creations.

Although this branch of drawing may be visually less attractive, it is essential in the study and application of fashion design, in the introduction to pattern design, and in tailoring. It is not just concerned with showing current fashion trends, but rather with teaching appropriate techniques for putting into practice and giving expression to personal creativity in a clear and schematic manner.

This book offers many varieties and models of each type of garment: trousers, blouses, jackets, shirts, underwear and accessories. It also gathers together trends in costumes throughout the history of clothing. For example, in the section on trousers the shapes and characteristics of each typology are illustrated, from the most formal and commonplace to the most diverse, for instance fishing trousers, baggy trousers, skirt trousers and pirate trousers.

Everyone in the fashion world knows that what really confer a personal and distinctive aesthetic are accessories. For this reason, and because they play a fundamental role in the history of fashion throughout the centuries, a great variety of hats, shoes, belts, and purses are also included. These items are undoubtedly necessary for achieving a universal and stylistically complete creation.

Thanks to the numerous drawings that appear in these pages, the reader will be able to undertake research to stimulate their creativity and create multiple designs, as well as paying attention to all those details that normally pass unnoticed but that are extremely useful at the time of showing the shapes of the garments or the hang and personality of the materials – the tracing of the seams, the pleats or the creases.

This is a basic and practical book that feeds the imagination and helps to capture on paper every design in the closet.

Collars
Cuffs
Trimmings
Necklines

Shirt collar trims
Front and side view of a deep V-neck, with
backstitch and buttonhole trimmings

Collars

Polo shirt collar with button
This collar is somewhere between the formal and
the informal

Double-sided baby collar
Also known as the Peter Pan collar, it is made from
two pieces of cloth that face each other and end in
round edges

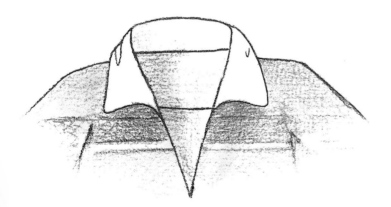

Polo neck collar open in a V
Variant of the traditional polo neck that substitutes
the buttons with a triangular piece of cloth

Tracksuit collar, sports garment
Round collar that closes with the same zip
as the jacket

Buttoned turtle neck
Goes above the base of the neck and closes
with buttons behind or at the sides

Foulard
This collar incorporates a long, narrow
piece of cloth, gauze, or another light
material

Scarf
Represented as a long, wide piece of material
that encircles the neck

Bow
A longer foulard that ends in a
voluminous knot

Draped neck
Neckline with a round or pointed cut that turns
forward with a certain volume

Bandana
Of Hindu origin (*bandhana*, 'to tie'), this
triangle falls over the neckline towards the
line of the bust

V-shaped collar with zip
The most usual option for knitted sweaters

Elastic boat neck
Neckline hangs straight from shoulder to shoulder
following the line of the collar bone

Plain lapel collar with button
Front part of the jacket, or coat, which is folded
and sewn to the collar

Lapel collar with button
The varieties of the style can be seen in trimmings
such as buttons or different textures

Double wrapover collar with button panel
Piece strengthened with double-width fabric or by
a material that is thicker than that of the jacket

Collar with an arabesque motif
Outlined by some elements of Arabic trims,
composed of geometric figures, leaf motifs and
ribbons

Polo neck collar with hook and eye
The characteristic polo neck collar and the feature
that distinguishes it from T-shirts

Large scoop collar with a bow
Leaves the shoulders bare and is finished off with a
figurative or genuine bow

Cardigan
Jacket of wool or another fabric, without a collar
and fastened at the front

Cuffs

Pointed cuff
The most traditional and elegant, and the favourite
with formal wear such as a dinner jacket

Turned-up cuff
Has its origin in the cuffs of masculine riding jackets
of the eighteenth century

Cuff fastened with studs
One part of the cuff has been left open so that the
fasteners can be seen

Cuff with cropped corners
One of the most popular sleeve endings for shirts

Elastic cuff
Characteristic of tracksuits, sweaters and jackets

Shirt cuff in a wave form
Commonly used form for sleeve endings in blouses

Trimmings

Shirt sleeve trim
The illustration focuses on the structural parts of the garment

Half-sleeved shirt trim with bent elbow
Shows how the garment behaves with body movement

Full skirt pleats trim
Folds are sewn tightly over the hips: soft pleats give fullness to the skirt

Wide turned-up collar trim
Wider and higher than normal, this collar has a decorative purpose

Long collar trim
Normally used in tight-fitting dresses and coats; was very fashionable in the 1920s

Lace-up trim for bodice
The lace-up regulates the pressure of the corset

Pleats trim for pleated trousers
The pleats below the waistband give fullness and
freedom of movement

Collar with zip
Shown half open to allow the tailoring trims from
inside and outside to be seen

Knot trim
This detail is important when the knot forms part
of the design of the garment or the accessory

Button fastening trim on the collar of a jacket
The high seam included the buttons in feminine
clothes from 1930 onwards; prior to that they
were used only in men's garments

Necklines

Square neck
Known also as a French neckline; frequently seen in feminine T-shirts

Sweetheart neckline
Follows the line of the bust, ending in a point at the heart; widely used in romantic dresses

Imperial neckline
Falls toward the bust in the shape of a point or V; emphasizes generous busts and makes the shoulders stand out

Long V-shaped neck
This neckline, which ends just above the waist, has been a favourite for designers in recent years

Collaret trim
Single gathered piece of cloth that falls over the shoulders and the bust; can also be used with a square neckline

Tear neckline
Falls in a rounded shape from the shoulders and ends in an wavy point at the level of the bust; its shape is like an inverted tear

Boat neck
Forms a straight line that goes from the shoulders or the collar bones; is elegant and discreet

Long collar
Neckline with a round or pointed cut, also known as a draped neck because of the folds that provide its volume

Cowl collar
Represented as a wider than normal neckline

Neckline with a collar gathered with cord
Widely used in peasant-style or romantic blouses

T-shirts
Shirts
Blouses
Sweaters

T-shirt
This versatile garment has become a staple of the
contemporary wardrobe

T-shirt with round collar
The most classic and widely used to give a sporty
look

Wrapover T-shirt with a V-neck
The inspiration for these T-shirts is the kimono

Shirts

Shirt with a yoke
The yoke is the upper part of the shirt or dress
to which the neck, sleeves and the rest of the
garment are attached

Straight shirt
Clean lines giving a basic style

Sleeveless shirt with a collar with pointed lapels
Its shape has evolved from the masculine waistcoat

Dress shirt
White or very pale in colour, this shirt must have a low collar for the bow tie and a double cuff for the cuff links

Shirt with mandarin collar
Heavily influenced by the popular Chinese style

Oriental-style shirt
The trimming of a line of buttons along the
shoulder and the mandarin collar reveal an
Oriental influence

Denim shirt with a pocket
Has the pattern of a traditional shirt, but the
pocket and the epaulettes are essential for defining
a casual air

Blouses

Gypsy
Blouse with a Bohemian inspiration that, because of
its structure, requires definition in its outline

Blouse with a knotted collar
Type of blouse that originates from a collar trim

Peasant-style blouse
Associated with romantic styles, and for this reason is drawn with diaphanous lines and gathers

Blouse with frills
Blouse with thin frontal strips that are sewn in pleats and shaped like small flounces

Wide blouse with
Shown here with
which give it volu

Lace blouse with front panel
The lace combines easily with any kind of fabric
and is often used in trimmings for both skirts and
blouses

Blouse
Traditionally a peasant garment. In the twentieth
century, this item transformed itself into a staple for
all occasions and circumstances

Jackets
Coats

Victo
Direc
is fitt
a hig

Leather jacket with zip
From motorcyclists to rockers, this jacket defines a
certain style

Jacket with tailored lapel
A T-shirt with rounded collar worn underneath a
jacket with tailored lapels creates a contemporary
look

Jackets

Jacket with round double collar
This warm garment is shown short and adjusted to the hip

Jacket with a dinner jacket lapel
Masculine garment developed from the cut of a riding coat; its unisex style means it is found in the wardrobes of both men and women

Jacket with fitted lapel
At the end of the nineteenth century, when women took up sports such as horse-riding or tennis, this garment became part of their dress

Jacket with a chimney collar neckline
Since the eighteenth century, when it was born in France as a garment for horse-riding, the jacket has evolved like no other article of clothing

Neat sailor-style jacket
Double-breasted gold-button fastenings
characterize this classic from the high seas made of
blue woollen cloth

Short parka with hood
Waterproof jacket originally used by skiers, with
the addition of leather to the hood

Jacket with pocket flaps
The pockets become the protagonists thanks to
the flaps that cover the openings

Denim jacket
Having seduced stars from the movies and rock-
and-roll during the 1950s, this jacket has long since
established itself as a staple of casual fashion

Double-collared three-quarter length parka
The puffed-out style suggests the quilted interior

Coats

Tailored coat with collar and lapel
The length of these coats does not allow for skirts or dresses that are longer than them

Coat with hood
This garment is a natural evolution from warm cloaks

Straight coat open neck with lapel
Warm masculine garment that can be worn instead of a suit jacket

Three-quarter length coat
A warm garment rather larger than a jacket

Long leather coat, front view
The seams at the sides and the collar create a lean,
vertical look

Long leather coat, rear view
This diagram shows the position of trimmings on
the back of the coat

Raincoat
The drawing shows the cape sewn on the shoulders, and the belt that characterizes this waterproof garment

Double-breasted raincoat with double button panel
Free version of a raincoat influenced by the design of warm coats

Wide fishing trousers
Quite apart from the shape that defines them, these trousers must maintain their length just below the knee

Tracksuit trousers with cords on the legs
The characteristic of these trousers is freedom of movement and the ability to alter the width at the bottom of the leg

Straight trousers
With typical masculine cut, straight vertical lines predominate in these trousers

Bell-bottoms
The trousers widen as they reach the bottom of the leg – a favourite in the disco era of the 1970s

Tracksuit trousers
Traditional representation of sports trousers

Pyjama bottoms
To distinguish them from the tracksuit a cord has
been added to the waist

Loose-fitting trousers
Garment with wide legs with gatherings at ankle level and pointed cuffs

Tracksuit trousers with cords on the sides of the legs
This innovative trim means that this style is often used outside of the gym as a part of urban fashion

Shorts with trimmings at the bottom
This garment is not now exclusively used on the beach or for playing sport; those with pure lines and restrained colours form part of a city wardrobe

Shorts skirt
Wide open skirt that is sewn down the centre like shorts

Skirts
Dresses

Full skirt
The spread is represented by the triangular shape
and the impression of volume

Denim-style skirt, rear view
The perspective from the back of this skirt shows
the similarity of its cut to that of jeans

Skirts

Plain asymmetric skirt
Modern variation of a traditional skirt

Full asymmetric skirt
The effect of movement is key in the
representation of this garment

Short plain skirt
With a straight cut, it reaches just above the knees;
consequently it is slightly longer than a mini-skirt

Trapezoidal shaped skirt with ribbon
Garment that is fashionable as a beach wrap and is
tied at the waist

Denim skirt with round pockets
The reinterpretation of the traditional denim skirt is achieved with minor modifications such as the shape of the pockets

Denim skirt with flounces
A way of achieving a lighter volume

Petticoat skirt
Represented as a wide skirt, generally white and
incorporating lace

Long denim skirt
With their minimal or non-existent spread, the
straight lines in this style predominate

Pleated skirt
From Coco Chanel to Wimbledon, pleated skirts have always been at the front of fashion

A-line skirt
André Courrèges and Pierre Cardin set this shape in the 1960s

Fashion Illustration: Plane Drawing

Bias skirt
Arose from a technique of the 1930s whereby the cloth was cut on the bias, allowing the material to fall in an attractive and flattering way

Cancan skirt with tutu
Takes its shape from the skirts of the famous dancers who performed in the dance halls of Montparnasse, Paris

Dresses

Dress with tucks
Dresses are ideal for ornamental options like this, which comprise a variety of hem lengths

Halterneck dress
Shown with an accentuated cut for the armhole at armpit level, also known as an American armhole

Dress gathered at the chest and waist
Garment with straight lines, very popular in the 1920s

Dress with a wrapover flounce
Inspired from old-fashioned underwear garments

Underwear
Accessories

Japanese wrapover bathrobe
Represented as a loose-fitting and comfortable
garment that brings to mind Japanese kimonos

Shirt-like bathrobe with yoke
Alternatives can be created with aesthetic options
such as a yoke or a tailored waist

Woman's bathrobe
Acquires a feminine profile because of the
trimmings and colour

Man's bathrobe
The wide sleeves and large pockets give it a
masculine character

Underwear

'Balconette' leotard
This garment has been designed to show off the figure, hence the seams around the hips, abdomen and bust

Sports leotard
Distinguished from the 'balconette' by its simpler neckline and absence of seams

Brazilian knickers
They cover slightly more than the tanga and less than conventional knickers

Knickers with a low waist
Pin-up inspiration for this garment that has a similar structure to old-fashioned French knickers

Triangular bikini bra with tie at neck
Fastened at the back of the neck with a knot or a
brooch

Sash-type bikini bra
Can be fastened just at the back and / or with a
knot behind the neck

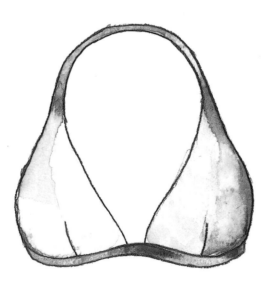

Triangular bikini bra
Its basic geometric composition has converted it
into a classic; the variants show themselves in the
ways in which it is fastened

Swimsuit with darts
Goes from the groin to the chest and
normally leaves most of the back uncovered

Shapely swimsuit
Most widely used for swimming as a sport; the
curved seams give a flattering shape to the figure
and facilitate movement

Bikini bottoms
The thin strips on the sides distinguish it from the
Brazilian knickers

Shorty low waist
Has the same structure as the low-waist knickers,
but the illustration gives it colour to distinguish it
as a bathing suit

Underwear Accessories

Accessories

Cap with military-style visor
The curved shapes of the crown and the peak, as
well as the colour, give it a military character

Unisex sports cap
Its fundamental characteristic is an enormous peak

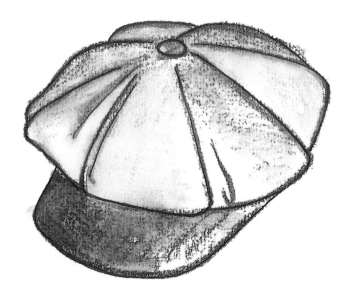

Wide cap
A direct descendant of the beret, it maintains its
basic construction with segments of cloth

Half-brimmed hat
The brim is rolled up at the back, represented in a
turn-up

Tweed hat
The drawing reveals the network of fabric threads, and suggests that it refers to a hat with a rigid structure

Sailor's hat
The curve-shaped crown characterizes this hat inspired by sailors' uniforms

Denim cowboy hat
Example that the cowboys adapted from the Mexican hat; it is identified by the wide brim, which is lightly folded at the edges

Flip-flop sandal
View from above the shoe, which consists of
just two pieces: the insole and the straps
that hook around the toes

Profile of flip-flop sandal
This allows the details of the design to be seen –
for example, the low heel and wide straps

Index